HYMNS FOR THE HOLLOW

Written by
Adam James Zahren

© 2025 Adam James Zahren

All rights reserved. No part of this book may be reproduced, stored in a retrieval system or transmitted in any form or by any means without the prior written permission of the publishers, except by a reviewer who may quote brief passages in a review to be printed in a newspaper, magazine or journal.

The final approval for this literary material is granted by the author.

Cover design by Michael Beas

ISBN: 978-1-962825-51-1

Dedication

This book is dedicated to those who've always believed in me - especially for Scott, my Dad, and Shelley, my Aunt. This book was made possible by the women of pop culture, and these words are for all the Little Monsters who still dance in the dark.

Hymns for the Hollow

Hymns for the Hollow Preface 5
Fallen 7
Crushed Dorothy 8
Fermented 9
Call Me Sister 10
Running 11
Pledge 12
Liquid Reflections 13
Ashes of a Polaroid 14
Formaldehyde Dreams 15
Formerly Blank Slate 16
Relics 17
Crumbling Cathedral 18
Fine Lined Caricatures 19
Hand Mirror 20
Melodies in Marble 21
War 22
Grown for This 23
Part Suicide 24
Mouth Cycles 25
Red Handed 26
Carcass 27
Last Goodbye 28
Requiem for an Echo 29
Pandora's Box 30
Blasphemous Body 31
Horror Tryptic 32
Transfiguration 33
Outside Inside 34
Ghost 35
Chains 36
Footprints In The Sand 37
Dirty Laundry 38
Hearing Drums 39
Friday Night 40
Entrenched 41
Sudden Change 43
After Our Last Goodbye 44
Requiem for My Inner Child 45
IV in Me 47
Mirror Voyage 49

Hymns for the Hollow Preface

This poetry collection explores self-identity, transformation, trauma, resilience, and personal mythology. Through evocative verses and various forms, these poems capture the complexity of human existence, blending raw emotion with fantastic elements to create a vivid, immersive reader experience. Each poem is a mosaic fragment of a broader narrative of struggle, survival, and the unyielding desire to reclaim one's voice in adversity.

At its core, this collection is deeply personal yet undeniably universal, offering an intimate glimpse into the trials of self-discovery and the process of healing our shared humanity. The poems move through an emotional spectrum—despair, defiance, vulnerability, and strength. The words on the page are an unfiltered reflection of the human condition, illustrating how pain can be both a wound and a catalyst for profound personal transformation. The speaker of these pieces grapples with their pain only to emerge stronger, empowered, and with a renewed sense of self.

This collection's defining characteristic is how it injects reality with fantasy and mysticism. The poet utilizes striking and surreal imagery to reframe lived experiences, often transforming pain into art. The author's interplay between the tangible and the ethereal creates a surreal reading experience where emotions are heightened, and reality bends into myth. The collection embodies the idea that storytelling, mainly through poetry, is a powerful tool for expression and queer survival.

The arc of the collection showcases themes of self-destruction and rebirth, underscoring the cyclical nature of shared human experience. These poems explore how people fall into the depths of despair only to rise again, reforged and renewed. Pieces delve into the weight of past traumas and the scars that linger when they heal; however, they also celebrate resilience, perseverance, and the ability to reclaim personal power. Through direct confessional tones or metaphorical narratives, the poet lays bare the complexities of human struggle, refusing to shy away from the raw, vile, and uncomfortable.

Music, mythology, and pop culture serve as key influences and run like threads through the collection, enhancing its depth and resonance. This collection uses music to add rhythm and cadence to the words, transforming each piece into a lyrical experience that feels nearly song-like. Mythological allusions make images timeless and universal, reinforcing that suffering, transformation, and redemption are woven through the fabric of human experience. At the same time, pop culture elements ground the work in a contemporary context.

The language throughout this collection is visceral and unfiltered, designed to provoke and stir emotions. Using striking, sometimes jarring imagery to confront themes and work through complex concepts, the poet does not hold back in exploring complex subjects. Yet, amid the darkness, there is light—moments of clarity, acceptance, and humor serve as reminders of the multifaceted, interdimensional nature of being alive. The juxtapositions of pain and beauty, suffering and survival, and growth and destruction create a dynamic reading experience that resonates long after turning the final page.

Structurally, the poems in this collection vary in form and style, further reflecting the chaotic yet deliberate nature of self-exploration. Some poems adhere to traditional forms, while others embrace free verse, allowing emotion to dictate the flow of words. This diversity in form mirrors the unpredictability of the themes explored—just as life itself is not uniform, neither is how it is expressed through poetry. Form truly unlocks function: the poet's willingness to experiment with structure enhances the collection's ability to capture raw, unfiltered emotions in their most accurate form.

The poems carry an undercurrent of defiance: a refusal to be silenced, a rebellion against social expectations and imposed limitations. The speaker asserts their right to exist fully and authentically, embracing their identity in all its complexity. These pages show fearless vulnerability and a willingness to confront external struggles and internal battles that often go unspoken. Unrelenting honesty gives this collection its power—it doesn't seek comfort but to challenge, provoke thought, and demand acknowledgment of brutal truths.

At the heart of these poems is a celebration of resilience. While the journey and arc of these poems may be tumultuous, ebbing and flowing between self-love and utter despair, an undeniable sense of triumph is woven through the series. Even in moments of despair, there is a recognition of strength—a testament to the indomitable human spirit. The poet does not dwell on suffering but instead transforms it into something meaningful, something beautiful. This ability to find power in pain and reshape it into art makes the collection not only deeply moving but also profoundly inspiring.

Ultimately, this poetry collection is an invitation—to feel, reflect, and embrace the messy, beautiful process of becoming. It is for anyone who has felt lost, broken, or unseen. It is for those who have battled their own inner demons and emerged, perhaps scarred but still standing. It is a testament that we are not alone, even in our darkest moments. The collection asks those who engage with it to turn the mirror on themselves and look inward. Through the power of poetry, we find connection, understanding, and the courage to keep moving forward.

Fallen

lightning-nailed to tree
wet metal and rust free

tethered tornado, stale-eyed hurricane
technically considered borderline insane

paradoxical infirmary
lined by yellow bricks
burst woven seams
splitting at the wrist

Crushed Dorothy

I walk down a beat-up yellow brick road
hearing all these budding flowers sing aloud
to bluebirds and buzzy yellow, magnetic bees
just passing through this reality entirely

as they fly, fly, fly
and time goes by bye-bye
with a tick and tock

but someone forgot
the clock hands demand
an hour passed, but progress
shan't stop, stop, stop–

infinity drops the proverbial ball, so the watch face
cracks like a mirror with seven years of bad luck,
but the hands go on twitching like a shoe-smashed
wasp seizing up on sizzling grey summer concrete

Fermented

inside a diamond–
deep within, ugly,
undercooked & wet

unprepared
for scrutiny
requires love
fused tending

scrapped & cut
into something worth
mentally masticating

Call Me Sister

screaming into a void
at the top of my lungs
under cathedral roof,
a nun crying out to
Heaven and Hell,

I begin to whimper
and break under
pressure: whip
cracks, plates smash,
debris pops

like pollen bubbles
in the spring

and my lungs go on
absorbing harmful
toxins and pains
this body aches

from bending
and stretching
the chords go
dry and sound

ceases all motion
passing by time

Running

Jazz magic in the air
smoke giving dada flair

pearls on necklaces belly dance
under fog laced bell air flare. Sweet
dances whisper to no one. Nobody

sees ankle ink
only energy

PLEDGE

fast fame and quick liquor
smashed bottle night terrors

discovered dismembered queer, burning embers
vibrate vibrant aesthetic maché

refute all restriction– unravel, unbind
crimp and kink, refine, realign

burn it, blaze it, feed it to flames–we can't
be silenced, our vocal cords won't go rust
you can not smite us with violent thoughts

Liquid Reflections

one lone blue fire in the kiln of my brain
solidifying miswired synapse highways
like a clay baked bowl with a hole or mug
lopsided– hardened memories malfunction.

i took my pain and transformed it to art
she stole my art and turned it into my pain
scripted old told lines, corset formed and
small, silenced, stoned, while ball gagged,

i became a wisp of a person–
drowning in liquor, smothering
smoky lungs, abusing bleeding
gums and a disrupted system.

these kinks in the wiring cause
memory shock. my body seizes
my eyes seem to stop and in my
mind the moment plays the hurt

of anguish, razor blades,
and shame. i say to myself
that i am alright, but i feel
i'm hanging off the wagon

sometimes by one finger
–brain alcohol embalmed

Ashes of a Polaroid

cigarettes sewn then to fingertips
with their crooked tree stump butts
burn these sacrificial bones for
fame, charisma, and young lust

my size nine shoe on a red brick wall
rough to the touch while toxic fumes
dance a waltz and sing lullabies–
people walk & gawk - I just puff.

The wind does my bidding, for I am
a God among men. The camera rolls
just for me and captures essential
beauty. I reach the stump just to spark

up again. Eventually, the pack
goes bupkis, filming wraps,
and feelings fade out. It all
burns up and blows away–

ash dancing in the synapses
of my skinny dipping brain

Formaldehyde Dreams

whispered moonlight pathways
cotton swabbed in empty pantries
left unspoken as communal secrets
like fairy ringlets left by little mushrooms all plentiful for the afternoon

dissociate the lemon's pucker lie like
a chicken pox and butter, chamomile
and seagrass bath all along an outer
pass as if the rays of sun sang out
and granted brilliance upon a scalp

alas the legends of old die young
and plenty fancied a new world tongue
if nature surpassed circadian rhythm
I'd be subjected to plentiful visions
my mind, it does wander and stagger

like lost harmonies I forgot to wager
come daylight come moon beams
come venus and mercury there is
nothing in this life that can save me

formaldehyde injects me in veins
that feel entirely new to me

Formerly Blank Slate
A Villanelle

---

mystic writings on my body, etched by
needles' ink, transforming epidermal
how the landscape fires under moonlight.

Adderall pulsing veins makes evenings fly,
and visions before me transcend where I fall.
Mystic writings on my body, etched by

Smoke and dust. This wretched fate is all mine
smoke puckers, lemoning lungs ring in the call,
how the landscape fires under moonlight.

It would seem there is nothing left but time,
although the clock faces are smashed, I brawl
mystic writings on my body, etched by

impromptu feelings of anger, lust– fine–
they simmer and bubble within me, crawl
where a landscape fires under moonlight.

All this manifests in thin, white lines
makes popper'd-gray-matter hit concrete walls'
mystic writings on my body, etched in
how the landscape fires under moonlight

Relics

the heart: bloody vomit, rotted brown boot
pressed to ground where worms fornicate–
step harsh! Flat line residual beats to pulp,
raw meat calling lame flies for early lunch

the brain: grey matter splayed out like puzzle
pieces bits jonesing for anxiety pills. pink fizzy
bits wet confetti stuck to walls, the lightbulbs,
caked into carpet like scrambled alphabet soup.

the hands: shattered ceramic porcelain bones
tarnished like forgotten silver left in a drawer
yellowed by scissor gripped compulsive smokers
I am kintsugi-ed. I transform into scribing cyborg

the feet: trudge forth like leather & lace
tread light leaving no prints on white sand
carrying the weight of shame and suicide
ankles imbued with fallen angel wings

Crumbling Cathedral

---

she says she's tired of screaming
at the top of her lungs, but I assure you
I've only just begun my requiem-
soliloquy for pain and suffering.

I am still falling down the rabbit hole
while furniture passes me by, lamps
bonk my body, and the light makes
fractured eyes. I vomit from vertigo

still falling down and as the fall
transpires, I feel myself healing
yet every hundred feet or so,
I get another whack or smack

and the blood comes gushing back
again, and I'm falling through
windows and smashing glass now
the red keeps pouring– I'm wearing

a thorn crown. Down my eyes
like tears, it all runs, until I'm
flat, a pancake, on the floor.
And I'm falling no more, alas–

Fine Lined Caricatures

---

look at my hyperbolized lines,
curves gesticulations birthed by ink
look how pigments contour the mirror

I think just call me Potsy Kleine, siren—
my name driven them to crash to shore

— make me mosaic, paint me pastiche
cultural hybridization & gaga feminism
masticated grace surmising the mystic.
Paint me French wearing that old party dress.

She's calling me bug but I hear bugs, so I eat carrots and wear blonde
hair, winged eyeliner shining brighter than technicolor:
the music's on, while the boys all stare

Hand Mirror

I am the sea witch, *bitch,* I have horns;
I command clouds; moon beams bend
for me; I know each sand grain by name.

The colors you see are of my own hues
there is nothing they haven't touched.

My veil hides my mask,
my mask hides the image of
another cyborg, vampiric woman
theoretics mixed with psychedelics

imbued with brilliance by definition the essence of absolute fantastical
immortal, infinite amounts of jaw dropping awesome

apples cure ailments,
spinning wheels heal,
wooden stakes answer
rouge silver bullets seal

the sky opens up, the rain starts to fall–
we are born to be born again and again.
I am the sea witch, bitch, answer the call

Melodies in Marble

rhythm lifts bubbles of bell jar glass
fingerprint *Grease* marked fierce and fast

these hands rise without second glance
I am the sound wave, I break into dance

my heart beats with bricks and songs—
machines hooked, leeching, into my veins
Venus screams my damned holy name
while Medusa's hair wraps my palms—

right there with them embraced by charm
this monolithic moment feels less like shame
I can rest heavy in their unbreakable arms

WAR

wasteful spender hypnotized sailor
medicated princess riding a chariot
starving artist pedagogic arsonist

it's gnawing at me, wafting
across this anorexic heart,
that empath covens covet

beats go on, time tapping out
rented-a-tent rented-a-tent
beats go on, time tapping out
rented-a-tent rented-a-tent

I line march eating
myself in the name
of love– always love

GROWN FOR THIS

I eat men in air gulps.
They leave me hollow
like a gutted pumpkin,
an empty watermelon.

An anorexic heart
tricked into calories
rejects tenderness
twisting her thorned

crown deeper into
flesh protected
capillaries lapping
up the stream

running down my mask.
They call me Scream
they call me VFT–
Venus Fly Trap, but
I am deadly nightshade.

They cut me down
dried me out and
jarred me. Now I
slip into their tea

burning them entirely internally
the whole way through, vicious
little screw– bitter, bitchy shrew

PART SUICIDE

i promised not to do it–
and didn't all the way,
but still i fucking did it–
only to parts of me.

Maybe they're not dead yet,
maybe they lie and wait
in pools of blood, in tombs in which
they're sealed with sleeping pills.

i never break a promise,
but i killed parts of me
i did it all with violence
and watched them all

bleed. Alcohol is sugar,
poppers used to clean,
razor blades and lemon
juice, with fire, gasoline.

i promised not to do it, but it's already done.
Cigarettes can't save me. Life isn't always fun

Mouth Cycles

candle melted down again
burnt coffee whiffs the air
black kettle water evaporated

again

so it goes

coughs out vile tar stained cilium
after picking up just another one
kettle whistles then– dry– again

Red Handed

---

i remember what love felt like in the stomach
and i recall the flutter in this chest, but there haven't
been emotions like that since– after college–

i killed that part of myself. i killed several
parts of myself. Pinpointing their ends
like needle hay, but i'm sure one of

those nights when i drank myself
into a pool of pop and vomit
or got face raped or woken up

just to be used contributed
to those little self-deaths.

i don't know their names
anymore, and i couldn't
see their faces. All i know is
that i killed them, those parts

of me and ate their bodies
by the weeping willow
naked at the local lake

Carcass

a deranged bird scavenging,
carrying an inability to remain

my own.
My own

bones holding feathers– listen
to the maggots all screeching

Last Goodbye

---

she lay– machine hooked and shuddered
– it nonconsensually oxygen-injected her.
room fading out with dissolving optics
– fixated on tubes, tubes, on tubes–

I held her hand. I wanted to sing,
something from *Joanne*– take my
hand. Just please, stay, *Marian*–

– but instead told her go, fly far
away– she deserved more than this
Hell– it was time to move on–

I didn't kiss her goodbye. Instead I
touched her opisthenar, caressed her
veins, and tubes, and skin, and tubes
and then walked away in so much pain

Requiem for an Echo

screams of teenage petulance
echo in my mind– *I'm no good*
– reverberations ricochet. All

acoustics ignore contemplating
grey matter asleep inside. Hemp
baked. Burnt like a cherry pie left
inside too long– oven coils glow

like dragon eyes guarding gold.
Silence these lambs, my own

tormented parts beaten, bruised,
and led to slaughter. I am fire–
phoenix or cat– time tracks that.

Pandora's Box

out of the darkness came my own heart
with the art of Medusa stained aortas
and pumping vessels glass-bedazzled,

and out of the darkness came lightning
scars embedded in capillaries, veins &
floating cells that scream under light–

candles hold me at bay. Garlic, a flame,
and I am a moth to the stake. Anti-vamp-
ire iris of the orchid original wasp, extinct

honey bee. My telephone won't stop ring-
ing, the ugliest sound– he said to me– enjambed
musically into my poetry. Help me understand

help me see the concave alcoves inside
my mind. Let music blare and sounds
ricochet like echolocation discovery–

I am god damn mythology
let them all learn of me when I am dead
and let them all mourn not knowing me then

Blasphemous Body

little tabernacle
upon an altar stone
stocked with eucharist
of heaven's only son.

Little tabernacle,
golden and exact,
you hold the wine,
blood-liquid life

tickle me divine,
down my gullet,
into stomach–
spread
thy kingdom come

inside me, fill me
up like you–
little tabernacle,
riddle me a chew

Horror Tryptic

I.
big mouth bite mark on my breast
bruises paint my tattooed chest

one said i deserved it. The other
growled he wanted to see it worse

One guy told me to eat garbage
while others say eat less.

II.
imagine a pane of glass
propped above the ground and flat

each of their pains a rock
placed upon its back. It cracks.

III.
i start to crave the pressure.
i begin to seek the weight

TRANSFIGURATION

I see screaming Rocky Horror
lips, teeth in the words before me

when I let my focus – like
wave caught, stuck driftwood,

and I think to myself
how beautiful things

can be when we just
let go – ebb, flow

and imagine
reality differently–

when we finally see
past the barrier and

bear witness to something
we were never meant to be

Outside Inside

they look out the window
elevated on a cat scratch tower

bound like princesses of the
forest or fairies kept in jars–

growth happens slowly
then all of the sudden

ones' tendrils reach past
the ground, another shoots

a furled tube straight to ceiling–
cinder blocks will stop it eventually.

There is one stuck on an island
with a face painted on her pot

and she grows quick as a slice
and sheds her lower leaves

She takes shape like a Truffula Tree–
robust on top with a bare trunk.

They stare from their coffins
out the windows and grow

without blinking–
sun always rising–
moon often smiling

Ghost

I leave men like air
blowing tree branches–

there for a moment
then off in the distance

where I'll find someone else
and tussle their hair

– I never save numbers
until they need blocked.

I give up on loving–
relinquish the thought.

My heart transformed from anorexic
to ectoplasmic. Look, Ma! it floats

Chains

leather and lace wash over me
like baptismal water ExxonMobil oil

I am a feather in dawn dish soap
cleansed for salvation: blind faith
and hope delay disappointment

some say, but to me,
hope is the key to unleashing
that thing perched, screaming
on your pale, palpitating chest

Footprints In The Sand

blood rolls down my leg
walking on the beach

crabs sniff, climb
scutterbug over toes

a million bits of sand on
soles. Where I'll walk

red coats run, gambling
with money they've lost.

The shower could not cage
me and the razor would not

take me, so I – along the shore.
Waves leave rabid, foamy residue.

Sharks smell me a thousand
miles away, they swim nearer

but they cannot reach me.
Here I stand– hungry, I am

numb and thirsty for more
blood, *mi amor*

Dirty Laundry

having fallen like a pebble
tossed to the wishing well

fresh kaleidoscope vision
as corrected prescription

mirages and illusions
will not escape me now

catch a rainbow, iris,
and photosynthesis.

Darkness can't consume
an atom powered light

nuclear the fallout
like a geyser spout

initiate the cycle,
and wash those
stains all out

Hearing Drums

nicotine and amphetamines
may have been the means

we used to find our wandering
brains. Academics assaulted

my senses, and I don't believe
in time. Watch the clock hands,

paint dries, and fall down on
your knees– deadlines come

and papers couldn't write them-
selves back then, so we stayed up

all night popping pills and smoking
reading books and writing. Dean's

List quality and then friendship
deteriorated – mental state de-

stabilized until – found a new
rhythm with one beating drum

Friday Night

skin tight
yellow leather
like banana
nylon peels
steam feather
stockings up
socks cotton
high knees
red eyes
magazines
razor sharp
people, please
kiss cheek
on lips– *oui*

glitter on the
serpentine
red carpet
movie scene
jazz floors
hotter rods
then you said
stay sharp
razor blades
and jean shorts
make the cut
patch them up
buttoned clutch
nobody touch–

no way
love hurts
bite marks
babysitter's
jean skirt
strutting with
concrete heels
clip-clopped
staccato feels
pitter-patter
big splatter
hands move
shattered clock
slow groove– *see*

Entrenched

it can not
be explained–

maim
crave–

how tattoos
can't come close

to source
tapping.

Needle pricks
sting like candy

compared to burns
festered by boiled

sugar. These innards
writhe and scream.

This pain
ingrained
makes

words fall short
& blood alludes

shame–
      delicious
      steeped release.

I heal tighter.
The hurt gets
soul
enjambed–

lost in translation
a wavering hand

lost and embedded
itch agonized aches

unrealized
stretch

Sudden Change

I saw the mountain move.
I watched it grow legs
and walk a few feet

toward the sunset
where the birds fly
in the distance. There

where the clouds
seem angry–
there where fire
just– *zap*– ignited.

I watched the legs step
in time– 1, 2 ,3– then
stop, plop, just there.

Eyes wide, cherry pie
jaw dropped, cod fish

I saw the mountain move.
Everything is different, yet
remains the same. I bore
the landscape shift, while

standing, breathing– in
and out– bathing with
the rain, I am still–
maintain

After Our Last Goodbye

hobble horse, along the path
as the bit your teeth do gnash

the carriage crashes
spills her ashes
the wind whiplashes

and makes a fog of me.
All around I see nothing

but bit of her inhaling me
I scream. I yearn her urn
but clumsily and blindly

buried it in mossy grass
and not far out at sea

I am sorry,
Mimi

Requiem for My Inner Child

if I were a little boy
I'd look at myself
confused & afraid–

5 foot 9,
follicles stripped

tattoos and tar
scarred lungs, big,
untamed kinky hair,

chipped front tooth
and imperfect gap

– if I were a little boy,
riddle me perplexed–
*How could I end
up this way?*

"Life,
I'd say
has a way
of shaping

Us in ways We can't predict.
The lies You're fed do not reflect
the ways people truly live.

But you must go on
believing in love,
and you must go on
believing in goodness,

for You are too sweet,
I'd say to me, to be told
how wicked things can get.

Go on and know
each tattoo and
cigarette fills a
form the universe

cut
once"

IV in Me

I.
sitting here under
another Chandelier
in the Haus of Gaga
where the magic all

happens on the hunt
success mixed with fun.

Look out Vegas,
here I come–

II.
I hear someone
reading the last
poem I wrote–
another voice says,

"Hey, Lady shut the
fuck up" and my
hat falls– first rain drop.

III.
I don't know etiquette.
I'm bad at boundaries.
I find it hard to walk
away when something
is happening. Why am
I this way? How can it
Be so? Oh, woe! I weep.

IV.
read me like poetry
and enjamb me just

right let me flow
into metric feet

and grant my stanzas
fine shape and light.

Grant me ability to
be artistry marble
carved majesty
like Michelangelo

made. Hyaluronic
and hypnotic siren
song I hum. I taste

like THC gummies,
lemon-lime soda,
and bottles of Stella.

I quit cigarettes but
vape like a cloud.

I strive to be a ripple
of sunshine– or a
radioactive butterfly

Mirror Voyage

locked away like a prisoner
confined, caged, and buried
lights growing, dusk showing.
Set me free, elusive key. Whole

geographics unmapped, this craft
Hades backed, my Hell navigated,
game set, match sail back and forth
— *lumos,* Pluto, *lumos.* We've got

to free the rest—

About the Author

Headshot by Jenna Ryan
(Instagram @jennaaryann)

Adam James Zahren (they/them or he/him) is a writer and multidisciplinary artist with a passion for storytelling in all its forms. They hold a **B.A. in English** from Allegheny College, specializing in nonfiction and poetry, and an **M.A. from Prescott College**, where they focused on social justice and community organizing.

Zahren's work has been featured in *Queer Studies in Media & Pop Culture*, where they co-authored the research piece **"Post-Homophobia Comes Out: The Rise of Mormon Polygamy in Pop Culture"** alongside professor Courtney Bailey. They also penned the homepage feature for *GagaDaily.com* celebrating **Lady Gaga's 10-year career anniversary**.

Beyond writing, Zahren has a background in performance, appearing as an extra in *The Perks of Being a Wallflower*. A lifelong creator and devoted cat enthusiast, they spend their time painting, writing poetry, crafting with their Cricut, and immersing themselves in music—often accompanied by their feline companion, Beau, who enjoys songs and head scratches.

Contact and Connect

Email– ajamesren.creates@gmail.com

Instagram– @ajamesren_creates

LinkedIn– Adam James Zahren

Writers Work– writers.work/ajamesren

www.ingramcontent.com/pod-product-compliance
Lightning Source LLC
Chambersburg PA
CBHW071148060526
44107CB00133B/596